Trials & Tribulations of Sports Bob

Trials & Tribulations of Sports Bob

Poems by

Sharon Waller Knutson

Cover design by Shay Culligan
Photo of Bob and cat, Axel, by Carole Brown
Wedding photo of Bob and Carole Brown by Morgan Lee
Photo of Butte, Montana, in the 1960s by Bob Brown
Photo of Carole Brown and kitten by Bob Brown
Author photo by Al Knutson

ISBN: 978-1-63980-034-6

Kelsay Books
502 South 1040 East, A-119
American Fork, Utah 84003
Kelsaybooks.com

For Bob and Carole

Acknowledgments

I'd like to thank the following journals for publishing these poems:

Red Eft Review: "Formaldehyde, Vinegar and Newsprint" and "The Call Never Comes"

Spillwords: "Sunrise Over Whiskey Jack Lodge"

The Song Is . . . : "Falling for Her," "Hermit Bob." "Photo of Baby Bob," "Sept. 5, 1964, Wisconsin," "Sports Bob," "The Innocents," "Watch Cats"

Trouvaille Review: "Pushing Eighty."

Verse-Virtual: "Aug. 5, 1962, Wisconsin," "First Memory," "Photo of Baby Bob," and "Tripping"

Contents

Photo of Baby Bob

Although he has the face
grandmas and mamas
pinch and pray
their daughters will marry,
in his black jumper
and gray sweater, his body
fattened up by his German
grandma and mama
who dote on this first born
of a farmer and a housewife,
shows he is no prima donna.

His eyes are used to the dark
and his nose tells him
something stinks, but he
doesn't know it's him.
He thinks it is normal
to live without electricity
or running water
and to get hosed off
at the car wash next door
when his father thinks
he smells too bad.

He pays no attention
to the stuffed bear plopped
beside him because he
is fascinated by the flashing
light that bursts out
of the big box on a stick
that makes him blink.

He doesn't know that
at only a few months old
when he gazes into the lens
he is looking into his future.

First Memory

He is two years old
and his grandfather
is taking a nap
in a large wooden box
in his living room,
packed with strangers
dressed in black.
He is pouting and running
around like a wind-up toy.
He wants his grandfather
to wake up and pick him up
and tickle his belly
with his beard. He wants
all those people to go away
so his mother will pay
attention to him. Most of all
he wants his grandmother
to stop wailing because
it is hurting his ears
and making him cry.

Feb. 1, 1959, Green Bay Wisconsin

It's the evening before
his seventeen birthday.
The Riverside Auditorium
is packed and pulsating
with sweaty screaming fans

as Buddy Holly belts out,
That'll be The Day
and *Peggy Sue* and he can't
believe he's in the same room
with his idol dancing

with a pretty hometown girl
he brings to the winter ball.
The Big Bopper and Richie Valens
are there too, but Buddy Holly
is the singer he has come to hear.

Six feet tall, he reaches
up and catches a Peggy Sue
45 RPM record tossed out
to the crazed crowd,
and being a gentleman

he hands it to his date,
which he regrets when
just two days later the radio
and TV announcers
shout, *Buddy Holly is dead.*

Mangled with metal.
Years later, he tries
to buy the record back,
but she says it's gone,
just like Buddy Holly.

Sports Bob

He is seventeen,
a six foot senior,
forward for Oconto High.
No. 44 on his back.
The score is tied
and Buddy Yeager

roars across the court
like a freight train
and he steps out
and his nemesis
slams into him, pinning
him to the floor. *Foul.*

The ref blows the whistle
and holds up two fingers
and he shoots the ball,
it soars and sinks the basket
as the crowd cheers
and his team carries him

on their shoulders to celebrate
beating their rival Oconto Falls
for the first time in six years
in their cracker box gym.
Snags the trophy for Captain
of the 1959–60 season.

Uniforms soaking wet
right down to the jock strap,
as snow and slush pile up
four inches deep on the football
field, they trail the other team.
Shiver and you are toast,

the coach shouts. He grits
his teeth and his father
tells him to quit belly aching
and start scoring. So he does.
He makes the touchdown
to win the game in Algoma.

He never misses a Milwaukee-
Braves game on the radio.
Freshman year, he hits a double
to win the game. His heart
breaks when his school
drops baseball.

A high jumper in track,
his muscular legs leap
over the high bar
to land in a sawdust pit
soft as feathers when fresh.
Hard as concrete after rain.

His golf coach would rather
play golf than teach it.
He is no Tiger Woods
as he hits and slices
and the ball slides right
past the hole, but he earns

nine sports letters despite
working in the lumberyard
and two factories and editing
the yearbook and his mother
harping on him daily,
Sports stink. Get a fourth job.

Formaldehyde, Vinegar and Newsprint

He scrubs, lathers and suds
skin, hair and clothes
in scalding hot water.

Still the stench remains
of the vinegar in the vat
as cucumbers

marinate and pickle,
at the factory where
he works after classes.

Of the formaldehyde
he uses to turn the dead
into mummies

and mannequins
to pay for college
and his room across the hall.

Now he wears the scent
of newsprint proudly
as he takes photos and writes

for his hometown weekly
sniffing the smell
of success on a city daily.

Aug. 5, 1962, Wisconsin

He is grilling hamburgers
in his back yard and his
mother is in the kitchen
when the policeman
hands him a telegram.
He shivers in the sunshine,
as he tells his mother,
younger sister and brother,
Dad's dead. Ejected
from his rig on the highway.
A pea farmer in a truck cut him off.
Massive head injuries.

He'll never forget
his uncle driving him
and his brother
to the accident scene
and stopping at a house
and introducing him
to the other driver,
who answers the door
without so much as a scratch,
Boys meet the man who killed
your father.

Or his mother shouting,
You're worthless
and will never amount
to anything, when his
salary doesn't cover
the bills. So when the
job offer comes, he is off
to Montana in his 1961
Chevy to prove her wrong.

Sept. 5, 1964, Wisconsin

Everything is white except
the croissants on the plate.
Perfume of white mums
turns St. Joseph's Catholic
Church into a garden.

He even wears a white tuxedo
to match his bride's organza
gown and both families
toast to the bride and groom,
Knowing this day would come.

But she is just his sister's
best friend and he the bossy
big brother until his senior year
when he notices she's all grown up.
But by then there is no time

for romance with college
and a job in Montana. Letters
fly. The phone rings.
He is smitten and buys.
a diamond ring and sends

it in the mail with a note,
Will you marry me?
And she calls and shrieks,
Of course, you idiot.
Soon they are on the road

to Montana, frigid
as Alaska and the Antarctic
But she's along for the ride
so she snuggles up to him
and turns up the radio.

The Innocents

Barely a bride,
she braces herself
against the wind
and frigid air
of this copper mining
town and snatches
up the stray off
the street. Barely
born, this silver
and black tabby
digs its claws
into the shoulder
of its new mama
and hangs on
as both of them
have no clue
that they have both
found their destiny.

Hell Hath No Fury Like An Athlete's Father

At the Montana State Basketball
Tournament, he reports in his newspaper
that the coach's son and star player
flipped the bird at the booing crowd.

He is sitting in the sports box
the next night when like Rocky
Balboa, the coach throws a punch
which he blocks with his arm.

When the game is over, security
guards escort him out of the arena
for his own safety as the coach
and his team shake fists at him.

When the coach and his team
burn his newspapers in a bonfire,
he dreams he is being barbecued
on a spit while the team cheers.

When he moves from Montana
to Minnesota, a boxing coach
calls him at home and shrieks:
How dare you write a story

about my son's opponent.
I know where you
live and I am coming
to burn down your house.

In his nightmares, he feels
flames burning his body,
sees the coach holding
a gas can and blow torch.

The Call Never Comes

He is working the night
shift at the Montana Standard
when his new bride
shows up with a draft
notice and a pepperoni pizza
they share with a reporter
who says, *You're going
to Vietnam buddy* and he
says, *You're next.* For weeks
the newsroom night shift
takes bets on when he will
be shipped off to bootcamp.
His editor remains calm
and quiet. He waits and waits
and when the call doesn't come,
he moves to Minnesota
for another sports editor job.
It isn't until he sees the Vietnam
Vets waving flags in the parade
in Rochester years later,
he realizes that if the call
had come, he too could be in
a wheelchair.

Jan. 12, 1975 Super Bowl IX

It's 40 degrees in New Orleans
but his feet begin searing like a steak
when he checks into the Marriot Hotel
three days before the game
between the Minnesota Vikings
and the Pittsburgh Steelers.

He isn't about to let sore feet
stop him from writing his pre-game
stories and covering the biggest
game of the year. By the time
the Steelers trounce the Vikings,

an army of fire ants devour
his feet and when he tries
to put his loafers back on
they howl like a coyote.

He squeezes shoes on and hobbles
through the New Orleans Airport
and boards the Chicago bound
Northwest Airlines flight.
As the plane soars in the air,

pain hot as a branding iron
presses against his arch
and his feet swell faster
than the ocean at high tide.
He tugs, but the loafers
remain cemented to his feet.

He flags down the young
blonde flight attendant
and she gets out scissors
and skillful as a surgeon.
she slices the shoes off.

He rides the plane the rest
of the way home and plods
through Chicago O Hare
Airport in his stocking feet.

Worshipping a Legend

It's the mid sixties in Butte, Montana
and he is announcing the names
of the players at the minor league
baseball game. *Here's Charley Pride,*
the pitcher for the East Helena
Smelterites. After the game,
the burly ballplayer introduces
himself, *It's Charley Pride. I sing*
country music in the local saloons.
Charley, now a hit on country radio
and at the Grand Ole Opry,
is performing a concert in the seventies
at the Mayo Civic Center in Rochester
and he is a journalist on the local
newspaper. The singer invites
him backstage and they reminisce.
In 2020, he watches TV to see
the superstar shriveled and shaky
receive a Lifetime Achievement award.
His heart breaks but not as much
as when he reads the headlines,
Charley Pride Dead at Eighty-Six
and writes on Facebook, *I just lost*
a very good friend today.

With a Little Help of Strangers

His 1971 Pontiac stutters
and stops on the shoulder
on the road between Rochester
and St. Paul on the way
to the Minnesota State
High School track meet.

He hitches a ride
to Little Oscar's Café,
where a patrolman sipping
coffee at the counter, looks
up. He tells the officer
he's a sports writer
with a stalled car
and a track meet to cover.

The patrolman drives him
back to his car, calls a tow
truck and follows
it to the repair shop, then
radios another patrolman
who is waiting twenty
miles down the road

and drives him another
twenty miles where
another patrolman
drives him to the track
and he arrives right
on time. After the meet,

a coach's wife drives
him to the Minnesota
St Paul Airport where
he rents a car and drives
home to Rochester.

Hauling Stepdad to the Hearse

It's 1980 and he drives home
to Wisconsin to cover
the Minnesota Viking-
Green Bay Packer
game for the Rochester
newspaper. His mother
has been married for eight
years to a guy who owns
a bar in his hometown.

A sports fan, his stepfather
smiles when he takes him
to the Super Bowl in Miami.
Before the Viking-Packer's
game, his stepfather's heart
stops beating in his sleep
and he calls the coroner.

Just like he did when picking
up dead bodies was his job,
he helped haul his stepfather
to the hearse but what he does
next is what he will regret
for the rest of his life: he drives
off to cover the game leaving

his mother standing there
on shaky legs on the porch
looking as lost and confused
as the day he checks her
into the nursing home after
her mind erases memories
and becomes an empty slate.

1980 Winter Olympics Lake Placid, New York

This is what he remembers:
Shivering for seventeen days
in the freezing temperatures.

Typing stories with
the windows open
in the Hungry Trout Motel

to let in the frigid air
as his fever burns
like a forest fire.

Hitch hiking to the arena
when the buses and taxis
are packed full of fans.

The passengers on the flight
home giving him a standing
ovation for being there.

Organizations asking him
to speak about what he saw.
And people of all ages

who don't know a hockey
puck from a basketball
recognizing him on the street.

But forever frozen
in his memory is the underdog,
US hockey team pulling off

The Miracle on Ice
and snatching the gold
medal from the hands

of the Russians and shocking
the world more than
earthquakes and tsunamis.

At the 1991 US Open Golf Tournament in Hazeltine National, Minnesota

Sunshine streams on the 11th hole
but as he and his friend Mike
saunter to the 12th hole,
the sky turns midnight black
and like a gigantic pitcher
pours water sideways.
The roaring wind drowns
out the screaming siren.

*Let's stand under this tree
until the storm blows over,*
he suggests. *Are you nuts?*
Mike says and they run
to the press tent for cover
just as shrieking ambulances race
to the 11th hole right where
they were standing.

They follow the ambulance
and see five golfers lying
motionless on the ground
as the press corps shows up.
*Lightning strikes four, kills
one,* the blonde broadcasts.

That could have been us,
he tells Mike. *It would have
been if we stood under that tree,*
Mike says. He guesses he should
thank Mike for saving his life,
but he is too busy wringing
out his clothes and Mike
is reaching for a beer
and sandwich from the cooler.

Mr. and Mrs. Rochesterfest

is what the press dubs them
for more than a decade. The Mrs.
organizes the summer carnival
rivaling a state or county fair.
Although she prefers being
the puppeteer and pulling
the strings, she smiles
on the cover of the local magazine.
Through a telephoto lens
he photographs the competitors
and the crowd to capture
grimaces and groans
as they run towards the finish
line, pull a rope, lift cars
and other heavy objects,
operate a hot saw
in a blizzard of dust,
chomp on turkey
legs and other delicacies
and try to talk
with their mouth full
of crackers. During those
summer days throngs
of people from all over
the country converge in Minnesota
but no one has as much fun
as Mr. and Mrs. Rochesterfest.

Sunrise Over Whiskey Jack Lodge

Ontario, Canada June 2006

The sun is a giant fireball
glowing in the gray sky,
reflecting on the water,
the empty boats silhouettes,

still as whiskey Bay
as he stands listening
to the sound of silence
as his fishing buddies

snore in their sleep
in the cabin behind him
not realizing this will be
their last fishing trip together.

Soon he will hear sloshing
of water as the boats
slide through the lake,
the snapping of lines,

the slapping of Walleye
and trout against the deck
the shouting and swearing
as they catch and release.

Then the sizzling of seasoned
fish in the frying pan,
the beer fizzling in the cans,
the laughing and lying

while they play poker,
the sun sets behind the bay
and the seven days fly by
like the great blue herons.

Then he's back to listening
to the shrill phones ringing,
the ref's and umps whistles blowing,
the balls cracking against the bats,
bouncing into the baskets,

flying across the football field,
the brawling, booing and cheering
and wishes he was watching
the sunrise over Whiskey Jack Lodge.

Bachelor Brother-in-Law

—for Lyle

Watching his wife's
baby brother turning
fifty, showing off gag
gifts, the giant clothes
pin nose plug, sweat
shirt with the saying,
Old Dude with Achy,
Breaky Parts, he thinks
of a standup comedian
whose body is falling apart.

But the brother-in-law
he knows is a serious guy,
with a ticker reliable
as a grandfather clock,
which is why a decade later
he and his wife worry
when the pharmacist
doesn't show up for work
or answer his phone.

He calls the policemen,
who peer in the window,
see his brother-in-law
sitting on the couch,
bang and holler, *Police open*
Up, and then kick the door down.

No pulse and a puppy on his lap.
The coroner says, *heart attack,*
which puzzles everyone,

especially his 96-year-old
mother-in-law who outlives
her only son by a year.

Watch Cats

For almost six decades
she has been rescuing
and watching stray cats.
However, Gold Nugget,
long gone, Axle and Boo Boo,
now the resident tabbies,
will tell you they have
been watching her
since they rescued her.
They watch her as she sleeps,
reads her mystery novels,
stirs the fondue in the pot,
views ball games and Dateline,
leaves for mass and the Mayo Clinic.
They're pretty sure they will
watch her until they die and then
she will acquire more watch cats.

Pushing Eighty

Gray sky peers through
the frost filmed window
as he reaches for his glasses
on the night stand
and tumbles from the bed.
His body is a boulder
landing with a thud
on the hardwood floor
like when as a boy
he falls from the Oak
as twilight blinks
through the forest
and slams against
the hard earth,
but just like then
he picks up his jigsaw
puzzle body and puts
all the pieces back together.

Tripping

He trips on a tangle
of cats and cords,
falls backwards,
twisting an arm
behind his back.
A blood clot
big as a baseball
forms on his bicep.
Under the aesthetic
he is a teenager batting
and burying balls
in baskets and holes
and packing a pigskin.
When he awakens
he is surprised
to find out he is alive
and his arm
is still attached
to the body he has
worn for nearly eight decades.

Falling for Her

He falls for her in high school
and falls all over her for almost
six decades of marriage.
But he doesn't fall head
over heels until sprinting
to his eighth decade
he loses his balance
and their nurse neighbor
hears screams and slips
out of her sickbed
and finds them sprawled
on the sidewalk, her femur
splayed and splintered
and his ribs rioting
and protesting
like the hawk and thrasher
in the oak tree in their yard.

Hermit Bob

Fileted from stem to stem
by surgeon's scalpels,
fingers and feet swelling
like yeasted bread dough,
he spends most of his time
on the second floor
of the house he has lived
in for five decades, mostly
in his office surrounded
by mementos of the sports
and music life he loves.
As the breeze blows the curtains,
letting in the sunshine, he is startled
by her footsteps, the flash bulbs
so bright even the striped tabby tries
to jump out of his arms,
but he holds on tight
because he knows the road is
going to get even bumpier,
and having lived eight decades,
he is prepared for whatever
life throws his way as long as
he has his computer and cats,
and, of course, her for company.

About the Author

Sharon Waller Knutson met Bob Brown in 1964 when he was sports editor, and she a reporter for the Montana Standard in Butte, Montana. When she left Montana, they lost touch and reconnected in 2020 on the Internet. After emailing daily for months, they decided to corroborate on Bob's memoir, with Bob providing the photographs and stories behind them. Sharon wrote the poems, and Bob edited the book.

Sharon Waller Knutson is a retired journalist who has been writing and publishing poetry for 16 years. She has published in numerous online journals and six poetry books, including *Dancing With a Scorpion* (2006) Moon Journal Press, *My Grandmother Smokes Chesterfields* (2014) Flutter Press, and *What the Clairvoyant Doesn't Say* (2021) Kelsay Books. She lives in Arizona with her husband, Al.

Bob Brown retired after a 43-year career as an award-winning journalist and photographer. He was a sports editor for the Montana Standard in Butte, Mt., sports editor for the Rochester Post-Bulletin, official photographer for the city's Rochesterfest, and editor of the Rochester MVP Magazine. When he retired from the newspaper, the mayor of Rochester declared it Bob Brown Day. He has been inducted in two halls of fame and won several trophies and plaques for playing sports in high school and reporting about sports events. He has traveled worldwide covering tournaments and games, including four Super Bowls and two World Series, and the 1980 Olympics. On Facebook, he has published over 500 stories of his interviews and sports columns. He lives in Minnesota with his wife, Carole.

Made in the USA
Middletown, DE
21 October 2021